KU-460-598

CONTENTS

05/07

UNIVERSITY OF WOLVERHAMPTON

Harrison Learning Centre
City Campus

RACE RELATIONS

CODE OF PRACTICE

For the elimination of
racial discrimination
and the promotion of
equality of opportunity
in employment

UNIVERSITY OF WOLVERHAMPTON
LIBRARY

WITHDRAWN

ACC No.

CLASS
331
.6

CONTROL

DATE
-1 SEP. 1994

SITE
DY COD

WP 0843799 8

PUBLISHER'S NOTE

The text of this Code of Practice, from page 5 to page 39 was issued pursuant to section 47(1) and (7) of the Race Relations Act 1976 and came into effect by order of the Secretary of State on 1 April 1984. The present reprint has been redesigned typographically, but the text remains unchanged, with the exception only of the following points:

1. New footnotes to paragraph 1.21 and the penultimate paragraph of the introduction, reflecting amendments to the law, have been incorporated.

2. Paragraph numbering has been dropped from the introduction.

3. Certain page references are different owing to new page numbering.

4. Some headings have been changed for the sake of clarity.

5. The terms 'guidance paper' and 'para' have been changed, respectively, to 'guide' and 'paragraph'.

UNIVERSITY OF
WOLVERHAMPTON
DUDLEY CAMPUS LIBRARY

© **Commission for Racial Equality**
Elliot House
10-12 Allington Street
London SW1E 5EH

First published April 1984. Reprinted 1991 and 1994

ISBN 0 907920 29 2

Price: £1.50

Printed by College Hill Press Ltd

Introduction

**Purpose
and status of
the Code**

S.47(1)

This Code aims to give practical guidance which will help employers, trade unions, employment agencies and employees to understand not only the provisions of the Race Relations Act and their implications, but also how best they can implement policies to eliminate racial discrimination and to enhance equality of opportunity.

S.47(10)

S.47(11)

S.32

The Code does not impose any legal obligations itself, nor is it an authoritative statement of the law — that can only be provided by the courts and tribunals. If, however, its recommendations are not observed this may result in breaches of the law where the act or omission falls within any of the specific prohibitions of the Act. Moreover its provisions are admissible in evidence in any proceedings under the Race Relations Act before an industrial tribunal and if any provision appears to the tribunal to be relevant to a question arising in the proceedings it must be taken into account in determining that question. If employers take the steps that are set out in the Code to prevent their employees from doing acts of unlawful discrimination they may avoid liability for such acts in any legal proceedings brought against them. References to the appropriate sections of the Race Relations Act 1976 are given in the margin to the Code.

Employees of all racial groups have a right to equal opportunity. Employers ought to provide it. To do so is likely to involve some expenditure, at least in staff time and effort. But if a coherent and effective programme of equal opportunity is developed it will help industry to make full use of the abilities of its entire workforce. It is therefore particularly important for all those concerned — employers, trade unions and employees alike — to co-operate with goodwill in adopting and giving effect to measures for securing such equality. We welcome the commitment already made by the CBI and TUC to the principle of equal opportunity. The TUC has recommended a model equal opportunity clause for inclusion in collective agreements and the CBI has published a statement favouring the application by companies of constructive equal opportunity policies.

A concerted policy to eliminate both race and sex discrimination often provides the best approach. Guidance on equal opportunity between men and women is the responsibility of the Equal Opportunities Commission.

Application of the Code The Race Relations Act applies to all employers. The Code itself is not restricted to what is required by law, but contains recommendations as well. Some of its detailed provisions may need to be adapted to suit particular circumstances. Any adaptations that are made, however, should be fully consistent with the Code's general intentions.

Small firms In many small firms employers have close contact with their staff and there will therefore be less need for formality in assessing whether equal opportunity is being achieved, for example, in such matters as arrangements for monitoring. Moreover it may not be reasonable to expect small firms to have the resources and administrative systems to carry out the Code's detailed recommendations. In complying with the Race Relations Act, small firms should, however, ensure that their practices are consistent with the Code's general intentions.

Unlawful discrimination

S.4

The Race Relations Act 1976 makes it unlawful to discriminate against a person, directly or indirectly, in the field of employment.

S.1(1)(a)

Direct discrimination consists of treating a person, on racial grounds,* less favourably than others are or would be treated in the same or similar circumstances.

S.1(2)

Segregating a person from others on racial grounds constitutes less favourable treatment.

S.1(1)(b)

Indirect discrimination consists of applying in any circumstances covered by the Act a requirement or condition which, although applied equally to persons of all racial groups, is such that a considerably smaller proportion of a particular racial group can comply with it and it cannot be shown to be justifiable on other than racial grounds. Possible examples are:

- A rule about clothing or uniforms which disproportionately disadvantages a racial group and cannot be justified.

---

* Racial grounds are the grounds of race, colour, nationality — including citizenship — or ethnic or national origins, and groups defined by reference to these grounds are referred to as racial groups

7

- An employer who requires higher language standards than are needed for safe and effective performance of the job.

The definition of indirect discrimination is complex, and it will not be spelt out in full in every relevant section of the Code. Reference will be only to the terms 'indirect discrimination' or 'discriminate indirectly'.

S.2   Discrimination by *victimisation* is also unlawful under the Act. For example, a person is victimised if he or she is given less favourable treatment than others in the same circumstances because it is suspected or known that he or she has brought proceedings under the Act, or given evidence or information relating to such proceedings, or alleged that discrimination has occurred.

The Code and good employment practice

Many of the Code's provisions show the close link between equal opportunity and good employment practice. For example, selection criteria which are relevant to job requirements and carefully observed selection procedures not only help to ensure that individuals are appointed according to their suitability for the job and without regard to racial group; they are also part of good employment practice. In the absence of consistent selection procedures and criteria, decisions are often too subjective and racial discrimination can easily occur.

Positive action

Opportunities for employees to develop their potential through encouragement, training and careful assessment are also part of good employment practice. Many employees from

S.37 & S.38   the racial minorities have potential which, perhaps because of previous discrimination and other causes of disadvantage, they have not been able to realise, and which is not reflected in their qualifications and experience. Where members of particular racial groups have been underrepresented over the previous twelve months in particular work, employers and specified training bodies* are allowed under the Act to encourage them to take advantage of opportunities for doing that work and to provide training to enable them to attain the skills needed for it. In the case of employers, such training can be provided for persons currently in their employment (as defined by the Act) and in certain circumstances for others too, for example if they have been designated as training bodies.* This Code encourages employers to make use of these provisions, which are covered in detail in paragraphs 1.44 and 1.45

Guides   The guidance papers referred to in the footnotes contain additional guidance on specific issues but do not form part of the statutory Code.

---

* Section 7(3) of the Employment Act 1989 has amended section 37 of the Race Relations Act with effect from 16.1.90. Section 7(3) now allows any person including employers (not just training bodies) to provide positive action training without the need for any designation as long as the criteria of underrepresentation are met.

PART I
The Responsibilities
of Employers

1.1 Responsibility for providing equal opportunity for all job applicants and employees rests primarily with employers. To this end it is recommended that they should adopt, implement and monitor an equal opportunity policy to ensure that there is no unlawful discrimination and that equal opportunity is genuinely available.*

1.2 This policy should be clearly communicated to all employees — eg through notice boards, circulars, contracts of employment or written notifications to individual employees.

Equal opportunity policies

1.3 An equal opportunity policy aims to ensure that:

a. No job applicant or employee receives less favourable treatment than another on racial grounds.

b. No applicant or employee is placed at a disadvantage by requirements or conditions which have a disproportionately adverse effect on his or her racial group and which cannot be shown to be justifiable on other than racial grounds.

---

* The CRE has issued guides on equal opportunity policies: *Equal Opportunity in Employment* and *Monitoring an Equal Opportunity Policy.*

c. Where appropriate, and where permissible under the Race Relations Act, employees of underrepresented racial groups are given training and encouragement to achieve equal opportunity within the organisation.

1.4 In order to ensure that an equal opportunity policy is fully effective, the following action by employers is recommended:

a. Allocating overall responsibility for the policy to a member of senior management.

b. Discussing and, where appropriate, agreeing with trade union or employee representatives the policy's contents and implementation.

c. Ensuring that the policy is known to all employees and if possible, to all job applicants.

d. Providing training and guidance for supervisory staff and other relevant decision makers (such as personnel and line managers, foremen, gatekeepers and receptionists), to ensure that they understand their position in law and under company policy.

e. Examining and regularly reviewing existing procedures and criteria and changing them where they find that they are actually or potentially unlawfully discriminatory.

f. Making an initial analysis of the workforce and regularly monitoring the application of the policy with the aid of analyses of the ethnic origins of the workforce and of job applicants in accordance with the guidance in paragraphs 1.34–1.35.

Sources of recruitment

Advertisements

S.29

1.5 When advertising job vacancies, it **is unlawful** for employers to publish an advertisement which indicates, or could reasonably be understood as indicating, an intention to discriminate against applicants from a particular racial group. (For exceptions see the Race Relations Act.)

1.6 It is therefore recommended that:

a. Employers should not confine advertisements unjustifiably to those areas or publications which would exclude or disproportionately reduce the numbers of applicants of a particular racial group:

b. Employers should avoid prescribing requirements such as length of residence or experience in the UK and where a particular qualification is required it should be made clear that a fully comparable qualification obtained overseas is as acceptable as a UK qualification.

1.7 In order to demonstrate their commitment to equality of opportunity it is recommended that where employers send literature to applicants, this should include a statement that they are equal opportunity employers.

Employment agencies

S.30

1.8 When recruiting through employment agencies, job centres, careers offices and schools, **it is unlawful** for employers:

a. To give instructions to discriminate, for example by indicating that certain groups will or will not be preferred. (For exceptions see the Race Relations Act.)

S.31 b. To bring pressure on them to discriminate against members of a particular racial group. (For exceptions, see the Race Relations Act.)

1.9 In order to avoid indirect discrimination it is recommended that employers should not confine recruitment unjustifiably to those agencies, job centres, careers offices and schools which, because of their particular source of applicants, provide only or mainly applicants of a particular racial group.

Other sources **1.10 It is unlawful** to use recruitment methods which exclude or disproportionately reduce the numbers of applicants of a particular racial group and which cannot be shown to be justifiable. It is therefore recommended that employers should **not** recruit through the following methods:

a. Recruitment, solely or in the first instance, through the recommendations of existing employees where the workforce concerned is wholly or predominantly white or black and the labour market is multi-racial.

b. Procedures by which applicants are mainly or wholly supplied through trade unions where this means that only members of a particular racial group, or a disproportionately high number of them, come forward.

Sources for promotion
and training
S.4 &
S.28
1.11 It is unlawful for employers to restrict access to opportunities for promotion or training in a way which is discriminatory. It is therefore recommended that:

14

a. Job and training vacancies and the application procedure should be made known to all eligible employees, and not in such a way as to exclude or disproportionately reduce the numbers of applicants from a particular racial group.

Selection processes

1.12 It is unlawful to discriminate,* not only in recruitment, promotion, transfer and training, but also in the arrangements made for recruitment and in the ways of affording access to opportunities for promotion, transfer or training.

Selection criteria and tests

S.4 & S.28

1.13 In order to avoid direct or indirect discrimination, it is recommended that selection criteria and tests are examined to ensure that they are related to job requirements and are not unlawfully discriminatory (See also p 7.) For example:

a. A standard of English higher than that needed for the safe and effective performance of the job or clearly demonstrable career pattern should not be required, or a higher level of education qualification than is needed.

b. In particular, employers should not disqualify applicants because they are unable to complete an application form unassisted unless personal completion of the form is a valid test of the standard of English required for safe and effective performance of the job.

---

* It should be noted that discrimination in selection to achieve 'racial balance' is not allowed. The clause in the 1968 Race Relations Act which allowed such discrimination for the purpose of securing or preserving a reasonable balance of persons of different racial groups in the establishment is not included in the 1976 Race Relations Act.

c. Overseas degrees, diplomas and other qualifications which are comparable with UK qualifications should be accepted as equivalents, and not simply be assumed to be of an inferior quality.

d. Selection tests which contain irrelevant questions or exercises on matters which may be unfamiliar to racial minority applicants should not be used (for example, general knowledge questions on matters more likely to be familiar to indigenous applicants.)

e. Selection tests should be checked to ensure that they are related to the job's requirements, i.e. an individual's test marking should measure ability to do or train for the job in question.

Treatment of applicants

1.14 In order to avoid direct or indirect discrimination it is recommended that:

Shortlisting, interviewing and selection

a. Gate, reception and personnel staff should be instructed not to treat casual or formal applicants from particular racial groups less favourably than others. These instructions should be confirmed in writing.

b. In addition, staff responsible for shortlisting, interviewing and selecting candidates should be:

● clearly informed of selection criteria and of the need for their consistent application;

● given guidance or training on the effects which generalised assumptions and prejudices about race can have on selection decisions;

- made aware of the possible misunderstandings that can occur in interviews between persons of different cultural background.

c. Wherever possible, shortlisting and interviewing should not be done by one person alone but should at least be checked at a more senior level.

Genuine occupational qualification

S.5
S.5(2)(d)

1.15 Selection on racial grounds is allowed in certain jobs where being of a particular racial group is a genuine occupational qualification for that job. An example is where the holder of a particular job provides persons of a racial group with personal services promoting their welfare, and those services can most effectively be provided by a person of that group.

Transfers and training

S.4(2)(b)

1.16 In order to avoid direct or indirect discrimination it is recommended that:

a. Staff responsible for selecting employees for transfer to other jobs should be instructed to apply selection criteria without unlawful discrimination.

b. Industry or company agreements and arrangements of custom and practice on job transfers should be examined and amended if they are found to contain requirements or conditions which appear to be indirectly discriminatory. For example, if employees of a particular racial group are concentrated in particular sections, the transfer arrangements should be examined to see if they are unjustifiably and unlawfully restrictive and amended if necessary.

c. Staff responsible for selecting employees for training, whether induction, promotion or skill training should be instructed not to discriminate on racial grounds.

d. Selection criteria for training opportunities should be examined to ensure that they are not indirectly discriminatory.

Dismissal (including redundancy) and other detriment
S.4(2)(c)

1.17 It is unlawful to discriminate on racial grounds in dismissal, or other detriment to an employee.

It is therefore recommended that:

a. Staff responsible for selecting employees for dismissal, including redundancy, should be instructed not to discriminate on racial grounds.

b. Selection criteria for redundancies should be examined to ensure that they are not indirectly discriminatory.

Performance appraisals
S.4(2)

1.18 It is unlawful to discriminate on racial grounds in appraisals of employee performance.

1.19 It is recommended that:

a. Staff responsible for performance appraisals should be instructed not to discriminate on racial grounds.

b. Assessment criteria should be examined to ensure that they are not unlawfully discriminatory.

Terms of employment, benefits, facilities and services
S.4(2)

1.20 **It is unlawful to** discriminate on racial grounds in affording terms of employment and providing benefits, facilities and services for employees. It is therefore recommended that:

a. All staff concerned with these aspects of employment should be instructed accordingly.

b. The criteria governing eligibility should be examined to ensure that they are not unlawfully discriminatory.

1.21 In addition, employees may request extended leave from time to time in order to visit relations in their countries of origin or who have emigrated to other countries. Many employers have policies which allow annual leave entitlement to be accumulated, or extra unpaid leave to be taken to meet these circumstances. Employers should take care to apply such policies consistently and without unlawful discrimination.

Grievance, disputes and disciplinary procedures
S.4(2) &
S.2

1.22 **It is unlawful** to discriminate in the operation of grievance, disputes and disciplinary procedures, for example by victimising an individual through disciplinary measures because he or she has complained about racial discrimination, or given evidence about such a complaint. Employers should not ignore or treat lightly grievances from members of particular racial groups on the assumption that they are over-sensitive about discrimination.

1.23 It is recommended that in applying disciplinary procedures consideration should be given to the possible effect on an employee's behaviour of the following:

- Racial abuse or other racial provocation.

- Communication and comprehension difficulties.

- Differences in cultural background or behaviour.

Cultural and religious needs

1.24   Where employees have particular cultural and religious needs which conflict with existing work requirements, it is recommended that employers should consider whether it is reasonably practicable to vary or adapt these requirements to enable such needs to be met. For example, it is recommended that they should not refuse employment to a turbanned Sikh because he could not comply with unjustifiable uniform requirements.*

Other examples of such needs are:

a.   Observance of prayer times and religious holidays.**

b.   Wearing of dress such as sarees and the trousers worn by Asian women.

---

*   S.11 of the Employment Act 1989 exempts turban wearing Sikhs from any requirements to wear safety helmets on a construction site. Where a turban wearing Sikh is injured on a construction site liability for injuries is restricted to the injuries that would have been sustained if the Sikh had been wearing a safety helmet.

S.12 of the Employment Act provides that if, despite S.11, an employer requires a turban wearing Sikh to wear other protective headgear such as a safety helmet on a construction site, the employer will not be able to argue that this is a justifiable requirement in any proceedings under the Race Relations Act to determine whether or not it constitutes indirect racial discrimination.

** The CRE has issued a guide entitled *Religious Observance by Muslim Employees.*

1.25 Although the Act does not specifically cover religious discrimination, work requirements would generally be unlawful if they have a disproportionately adverse effect on particular racial groups and cannot be shown to be justifiable.*

Communications and language training for employees

1.26 Although there is no legal requirement to provide language training, difficulties in communication can endanger equal opportunity in the workforce. In addition, good communications can improve efficiency, promotion prospects and safety and health and create a better understanding between employers, employees and unions. Where the workforce includes current employees whose English is limited it is recommended that steps are taken to ensure that communications are as effective as possible.

1.27 These should include, where reasonably practicable:

a   Provision of interpretation and translation facilities, for example, in the communication of grievance and other procedures, and of terms of employment.

b.   Training in English language and in communication skills.**

---

* Genuinely necessary safety requirements may not constitute unlawful discrimination.

** Industrial language training is provided by a network of local education authority units throughout the country. Full details of the courses and the comprehensive services offered by these units are available from the National Centre for Industrial Language Training, The Havelock Centre, Havelock Road, Southall, Middx.

c. Training for managers and supervisors in the background and culture of racial minority groups.

d. The use of alternative or additional methods of communication, where employees find it difficult to understand health and safety requirements, for example.

- Safety signs; translations of safety notices.

- Instructions through interpreters.

- Instruction combined with industrial language training.

Instructions and pressure to discriminate

1.28 **It is unlawful to** instruct or put pressure on others to discriminate on racial grounds.

a. An example of an unlawful instruction is:

S.30

- An instruction from a personnel or line manager to junior staff to restrict the numbers of employees from a particular racial group in any particular work.

S.31

b. An example of pressure to discriminate is:

- An attempt by a shop steward or group of workers to induce an employer not to recruit members of particular racial groups, for example by threatening industrial action.

1.29 **It is also unlawful** to discriminate in response to such instructions or pressure.

1.30 The following recommendations are made to avoid unlawful instructions and pressure to discriminate:

a. Guidance should be given to all employees, and particularly those in positions of authority or influence, on the relevant provisions of the law.

b. Decision-makers should be instructed not to give way to pressure to discriminate.

c. Giving instructions or bringing pressure to discriminate should be treated as a disciplinary offence.

Victimisation

S.2

1.31 It is unlawful to victimise individuals who have made allegations or complaints of racial discrimination or provided information about such discrimination, for example, by disciplining them or dismissing them. (See also page 8.)

1.32 It is recommended that guidance on this aspect of the law should be given to all employees and particularly to those in positions of influence or authority.

Monitoring equal opportunity*

1.33 It is recommended that employers should regularly monitor the effects of selection decisions and personnel practices and procedures in order to assess whether equal opportunity is being achieved.

1.34 The information needed for effective monitoring may be obtained in a number of ways. It will best be provided by records showing the ethnic origins of existing employees and job applicants. It is recognised that the need for detailed information and the

---

* See the CRE's guide on *Monitoring an Equal Opportunity Policy.*

methods of collecting it will vary according to the circumstances of individual establishments. For example, in small firms or in firms in areas with little or no racial minority settlement it will often be adequate to assess the distribution of employees from personal knowledge and visual identification.

1.35 It is open to employers to adopt the method of monitoring which is best suited to their needs and circumstances, but whichever method is adopted, they should be able to show that it is effective. In order to achieve the full commitment of all concerned the chosen method should be discussed and agreed, where appropriate, with trade union or employee representatives.

1.36 Employers should ensure that information on individuals' ethnic origins is collected for the purpose of monitoring equal opportunity alone and is protected from misuse.

1.37 The following is the comprehensive method recommended by the CRE.*

Analyses should be carried out of:

a. The ethnic composition of the workforce of each plant, department, section, shift and job category, and changes in distribution over periods of time.

b. Selection decisions for recruitment, promotion, transfer and training, according to the racial group of candidates, and reasons for these decisions.

---

* This is outlined in detail in *Monitoring an Equal Opportunity Policy*.

1.38 Except in cases where there are large numbers of applicants and the burden on resources would be excessive, reasons for selection and rejection should be recorded at each stage of the selection process, e.g. initial shortlisting and final decisions. Simple categories of reasons for rejection should be adequate for the early sifting stages.

1.39 Selection criteria and personnel procedures should be reviewed to ensure that they do not include requirements or conditions which constitute or may lead to unlawful indirect discrimination.

1.40 This information should be carefully and regularly analysed and, in order to identify areas which may need particular attention, a number of key questions should be asked.

1.41 Is there evidence that individuals from any particular racial group:

a. Do not apply for employment or promotion, or that fewer apply than might be expected?

b. Are not recruited or promoted at all, or are appointed in a significantly lower proportion than their rate of application?

c. Are underrepresented in training or in jobs carrying higher pay, status or authority?

d. Are concentrated in certain shifts, sections or departments?

S.4 & S.28 **1.42** If the answer to any of these questions is yes, the reasons for this should be investigated. If direct or indirect discrimination is found action must be taken to end it immediately.

1.43 It is recommended that deliberate acts of unlawful discrimination by employees are treated as disciplinary offences.

Positive action*

S.38

1.44 Although they are not legally required, positive measures are allowed by the law to encourage employees and potential employees and provide training for employees who are members of particular racial groups which have been underrepresented** in particular work. (See also page 8.) Discrimination at the point of selection for work, however, is not permissible in these circumstances.

1.45 Such measures are important for the development of equal opportunity. It is therefore recommended that, where there is underrepresentation of particular racial groups in particular work, the following measures should be taken wherever appropriate and reasonably practicable:

a. Job advertisements designed to reach members of these groups and to encourage their applications: for example, through the use of the ethnic minority press, as well as other newspapers.

b. Use of the employment agencies and careers offices in areas where these groups are concentrated.

---

*   The CRE has issued a guide on positive action, entitled, *Equal Opportunity in Employment: Why positive action?*

** A racial group is underrepresented if, at any time during the previous twelve months, either there was no-one of that group doing the work in question, or there were disproportionately few in comparison with the group's proportion in the workforce at that establishment, or in the population from which the employer normally recruits for work at that establishment.

c. Recruitment and training schemes for school leavers designed to reach members of these groups.

d. Encouragement to employees from these groups to apply for promotion or transfer opportunities.

e. Training for promotion or skill training for employees of these groups who lack particular expertise but show potential: supervisory training may include language training.

PART 2
The Responsibilities of Individual Employees

2.1 While the primary responsibility for providing equal opportunity rests with the employer, individual employees at all levels and of all racial groups have responsibilities too. Good race relations depend on them as much as on management, and so their attitudes and activities are very important.

2.2 The following actions by individual employees would be **unlawful**:

S.4 &   a.   Discrimination in the course of their employment against fellow employees or job applicants on racial grounds, for example, in selection decisions for recruitment, promotion, transfer and training.

S.33

S.31   b.   Inducing, or attempting to induce other employees, unions or management to practise unlawful discrimination. For example, they should not refuse to accept other employees from particular racial groups or refuse to work with a supervisor of a particular racial group.

S.2   c.   Victimising individuals who have made allegations or complaints of racial discrimination or provided information about such discrimination. (See also page 8.)

2.3 To assist in preventing racial discrimination and promoting equal opportunity it is recommended that individual employees should:

a. Cooperate in measures introduced by management designed to ensure equal opportunity and non-discrimination.

b. Where such measures have not been introduced, press for their introduction (through their trade union where appropriate).

c. Draw the attention of management and, where appropriate, their trade unions to suspected discriminatory acts or practices.

d. Refrain from harassment or intimidation of other employees on racial grounds, for example, by attempting to discourage them from continuing employment. Such action may be unlawful if it is taken by employees against those subject to their authority.

2.4 In addition to the responsibilities set out above individual employees from the racial minorities should recognise that in many occupations advancement is dependent on an appropriate standard of English. Similarly an understanding of the industrial relations procedures which apply is often essential for good working relationships.

2.5 They should therefore:

a. Where appropriate, seek means to improve their standards of English.

b. Cooperate in industrial language training schemes introduced by employers and/or unions.

c. Cooperate in training or other schemes designed to inform them of industrial relations procedures, company agreements, work rules, etc.

d. Where appropriate, participate in discussions with employers and unions, to find solutions to conflicts between cultural or religious needs and production needs.

PART 3
The Responsibilities of
Trade Unions

3.1   Trade unions, in common with a number of other organisations, have a dual role as employers and providers of services specifically covered by the Race Relations Act.

3.2   In their role as employer, unions have the responsibilities set out in Part 1 of the Code. S.11   They also have a responsibility to ensure that their representatives and members do not discriminate against any particular racial group in the admission or treatment of members, or as colleagues, supervisors, or subordinates.

3.3   In addition, trade union officials at national and local level and shopfloor representatives at plant level have an important part to play on behalf of their members in preventing unlawful discrimination and in promoting equal opportunity and good race relations. Trade unions should encourage and press for equal opportunity policies so that measures to prevent discrimination at the workplace can be introduced with the clear commitment of both management and unions.

Admission of   **3.4**   **It is unlawful** for trade unions to
members   discriminate on racial grounds:

a.   By refusing membership.

S.11(2)   b.   By offering less favourable terms of membership.

Treatment of members

S.11(3)

3.5 **It is unlawful** for trade unions to discriminate on racial grounds against existing members:

a. By varying their terms of membership, depriving them of membership or subjecting them to any other detriment.

b. By treating them less favourably in the benefits, facilities or services provided. These may include:

- Training facilities.

- Welfare and insurance schemes.

- Entertainment and social events.

- Processing of grievances.

- Negotiations.

- Assistance in disciplinary or dismissal procedures.

3.6 In addition, it is recommended that unions ensure that in cases where members of particular racial groups believe that they are suffering racial discrimination, whether by the employer or the union itself, serious attention is paid to the reasons for this belief and that any discrimination which may be occurring is stopped.

Disciplining members who discriminate

3.7 It is recommended that deliberate acts of unlawful discrimination by union members are treated as disciplinary offences.

Positive action

S.38 (3), (4) & (5)

3.8 Although they are not legally required, positive measures are allowed by the law to encourage and provide training for members of particular racial groups which have been underrepresented* in trade union membership or in trade union posts. (Discrimination at the point of selection, however, is not permissible in these circumstances.)

3.9 It is recommended that, wherever appropriate and reasonably practicable, trade unions should:

a. Encourage individuals from these groups to join the union. Where appropriate, recruitment material should be translated into other languages.

b. Encourage individuals from these groups to apply for union posts and provide training to help fit them for such posts.

Training and information

3.10 Training and information play a major part in the avoidance of discrimination and the promotion of equal opportunity. It is recommended that trade unions should:

a. Provide training and information for officers, shop stewards and representatives on their responsibilities for equal opportunity. This training and information should cover:

- The Race Relations Act and the nature and causes of discrimination.

---

* A racial group is underrepresented in trade union membership, if at any time during the previous twelve months no persons of that group were in membership, or disproportionately few in comparison with the proportion of persons of that group among those eligible for membership [S.38(5)]. Underrepresentation in trade union posts applies under the same twelve month criteria, where there were no persons of a particular racial group in those posts or disproportionately few in comparison with the proportion of that group in the organisation [S.38(4)].

- The backgrounds of racial minority groups and communication needs.

- The effects of prejudice.

- Equal opportunity policies.

- Avoiding discrimination when representing members.

b. Ensure that members and representatives, whatever their racial group, are informed of their role in the union, and of industrial relations and union procedures and structures. This may be done, for example:

- Through translation of material.

- Through encouragement to participate in industrial relations courses and industrial language training.

Pressure to discriminate

S.31

3.11 It is unlawful for trade union members or representatives to induce or to attempt to induce those responsible for employment decisions to discriminate:

a. In the recruitment, promotion, transfer, training or dismissal of employees.

b. In terms of employment, benefits, facilities or services.

3.12 For example, they should not:

a. Restrict the numbers of a particular racial group in a section, grade or department.

b. Resist changes designed to remove indirect discrimination, such as those in craft apprentice schemes, or in agreements concerning seniority rights or mobility between departments.

Victimsation
S.2

3.13   **It is unlawful** to victimise individuals who have made allegations or complaints of racial discrimination or provided information about such discrimination. (See also page 8.)

Avoidance of discrimination
S.31 & S.33

3.14   Where unions are involved in selection decisions for recruitment, promotion, training or transfer, for example through recommendation or veto, **it is unlawful** for them to discriminate on racial grounds.

3.15   It is recommended that they should instruct their members accordingly and examine their procedures and joint agreements to ensure that they do not contain indirectly discriminatory requirements or conditions, such as:

- Unjustifiable restrictions on transfers between departments.

- Irrelevant and unjustifiable selection criteria which have a disproportionately adverse effect on particular racial groups.

Union involvement in equal opportunity polices

3.16   It is recommended that:

a.   Unions should cooperate in the introduction and implementation of full equal opportunity policies, as defined in paragraphs 1.3 & 1.4.

b.   Unions should negotiate the adoption of such policies where they have not been introduced or the extension of existing policies where these are too narrow.

c.   Unions should cooperate with measures to monitor the progress of equal opportunity policies, or encourage management to introduce them where they do not already exist. Where appropriate (see paragraphs 1.33–1.35) this may be done through analysis of the distribution of employees and job applicants according to ethnic origin.

d. Wheɪe monitoring shows that discrimination has occurred or is occurring, unions should cooperate in measures to eliminate it.

e. Although positive action* is not legally required, unions should encourage management to take such action where there is underrepresentation of particular racial groups in particular jobs, and where management itself introduces positive action, representatives should support it.

f. Similarly, where there are communication difficulties, management should be asked to take whatever action is appropriate to overcome them.

---

* See paragraph 1.44 on positive action.

PART 4
The Responsibilities of Employment Agencies

4.1   Employment agencies, in their role as employers, have the responsibilities outlined in Part 1 of the Code. In addition, they have responsibilities as suppliers of job applicants to other employers.

4.2   **It is unlawful** for employment agencies (for exceptions see Race Relations Act):

S.14(1)   a.   To discriminate on racial grounds in providing services to clients.

S.29   b.   To publish job advertisements indicating, or which might be understood to indicate, that applications from any particular group will not be considered or will be treated more favourably or less favourably than others.

S.14(1)   c.   To act on directly discriminatory instructions from employers to the effect that applicants from a particular racial group will be rejected or preferred or that their numbers should be restricted.

S.14(1) & S.1(1)(b)   d.   To act on indirectly discriminatory instructions from employers i.e. that requirements or conditions should be applied that would have a disproportionately adverse effect on applicants of a particular racial group and which cannot be shown to be justifiable.

4.3 It is recommended that agencies should also avoid indicating such conditions or requirements in job advertisements unless they can be shown to be justifiable. Examples in each case may be those relating to educational qualifications or residence.

4.4 It is recommended that staff should be given guidance on their duty not to discriminate and on the effect which generalised assumptions and prejudices can have on their treatment of members of particular racial groups.

4.5 In particular staff should be instructed:

a. Not to ask employers for racial preferences.

b. Not to draw attention to racial origin when recommending applicants unless the employer is trying to attract applicants of a particular racial group under the exceptions in the Race Relations Act.

c. To report a client's refusal to interview an applicant for reasons that are directly or indirectly discriminatory to a supervisor, who should inform the client that discrimination is unlawful. If the client maintains this refusal the agency should inform the applicant of his or her right to complain to an industrial tribunal and to apply to the CRE for assistance. An internal procedure for recording such cases should be operated.

d. To inform their supervisor if they believe that an applicant, though interviewed, has been rejected on racial grounds. If the supervisor is satisfied that there are grounds for this belief, he or she should arrange for the applicant to be informed of the right to complain to an industrial tribunal and to apply to the CRE for assistance. An internal procedure for recording such cases should be operated.

e. To treat job applicants without discrimination. For example, they should not send applicants from particular racial groups to only those employers who are believed to be willing to accept them, or restrict the range of job opportunities for such applicants because of assumptions about their abilities based on race or colour.

4.6 It is recommended that employment agencies should discontinue their services to employers who give unlawful discriminatory instructions and who refuse to withdraw them.

4.7 It is recommended that employment agencies should monitor the effectiveness of the measures they take for ensuring that no unlawful discrimination occurs. For example, where reasonably practicable they should make periodic checks to ensure that applicants from particular racial groups are being referred for suitable jobs for which they are qualified at a similar rate to that for other comparable applicants.

Note
Information on the promotion of equality of opportunity in employment is available from the CRE's Employment Division and from the Department of Employment's Race Relations Advisory Service

COMMISSION FOR RACIAL EQUALITY

The Commission for Racial Equality was set up by the Race Relations Act 1976 with the duties of:

- Working towards the elimination of discrimination.

- Promoting equality of opportunity and good relations between persons of different racial groups.

- Keeping under review the working of the Act, and, when required by the Secretary of State or when it otherwise thinks it is necessary, drawing up and submitting to the Secretary of State proposals for amending it.

London (Head Office)

Elliot House
10-12 Allington Street
London SW1E 5EH
☎ 071-828 7022

Birmingham

Alpha Tower (11th floor)
Suffolk Street Queensway
Birmingham B1 1TT
☎ 021-632 4544

Leeds

Yorkshire Bank Chambers
(1st floor)
Infirmary Street
Leeds LS1 2JP
☎ 0532-434413

Manchester

Maybrook House (5th floor)
40 Blackfriars Street
Manchester M3 2EG
☎ 061-831 7782

Leicester

Haymarket House (4th floor)
Haymarket Shopping Centre
Leicester LE1 3YG
☎ 0533-517852

Scotland

Hanover House
45-51 Hanover Street
Edinburgh EH2 2PJ
☎ 031-226 5186

UNIVERSITY OF
WOLVERHAMPTON
DUDLEY CAMPUS LIBRARY